PAST SPEECH OF THE SEA

A Maritime History of Castlehaven

First published in 2003 by
Galley Head Press
Dunowen
Ardfield
Co. Cork
(023) 40881

ISBN: 0 9542159 1 5

Design & Layout
Dominic Carroll, Co. Cork

Printing
Colour Books, Dublin

PAST SPEECH OF THE SEA

A Maritime History of Castlehaven

TIMOTHY CHAVASSE

GHP
Galley Head Press

Contents

Fish Quay, viewed from rocks near Cat Island, c. 1865–80.

Foreword

When Tim mentioned to me that he was thinking of writing on the maritime connections of Castlehaven, I thought it was a wonderful idea. There is too little precise information about the villages on the Irish coast, and the fishing boats and other vessels associated with them. Castletownshend, at the heart of Castlehaven, has a particularly colourful history and a location unrivalled in beauty. Tim's detailed history of the boats that have sailed into Castlehaven vividly conveys the atmosphere of this unique inlet on the south-west coast of Cork. He has an intimate knowledge and love of the area, which is unsurprising since his family, long associated with the sea, lived first at Seafield and then at 'The Rocket House', built on the ruin of the old coastguard station.

My own memories have been revived by Tim's descriptions. My first impression of Castlehaven was during the summer of 1938 when we sailed in the *Shira* into that wonderful enclosed harbour, past Horse Island and the tower which Tom the Merchant built as a beacon, watching the village of Castletownshend slowly taking shape with lines of houses, groves of trees and the ruins of Raheen Castle at the end of the bay. Today, around 800 yachts visit the harbour annually; in those days, there were only a few fishing boats and we dropped our anchor in solitary splendour.

While Tim brings into his book important historical events connected with Castlehaven, his main concern is not with warships but with boats both grand and small. He describes the old fishing boats propelled by oars, and the long 'netters', with two masts and long bowsprits, carrying crews of twelve to fourteen men. The fishing boats have gone, although, in Tim's words, 'Their weed-covered timbers can still be seen sticking up through the mud at low tide, like the ribs of some prehistoric animal.' The pleasure boats included a type of craft unique to Castlehaven – the famous sailing dinghies belonging to the Ette class, designed and built by Jim Mahony in the 1930s. I know a little about Ettes, having been an inefficient crew in one during a local race, dancing round the harbour, pulling in ropes and avoiding the swinging boom.

Tim not only provides a comprehensible and readable account of local maritime craft, but includes material on many related topics, such as regattas, the names of boats and Nelson's Arch. There are also anecdotes, like the ladder of St Barrahane's, found drifting in the sea during the First World War and given to the church by a naval motor launch. This sort of detail makes the book a particular delight and, as a bonus, it is illustrated with superb photographs.

Peter Somerville-Large

Author's Note &
Acknowledgements

'Boating is the only thing,' said the Water Rat solemnly as he leant forward for his stroke. 'Believe me, my young friend, there is nothing, absolutely nothing, half so much worth doing as simply messing about in boats.'

from *The Wind in the Willows* by Kenneth Grahame

This is a short history about ships, boats and boating in Castlehaven from early times to the present. Although I have tried to be as truthful as possible, I apologise for any inaccuracies or omissions.

I would like to thank the following people who have helped me in so many ways while I was writing this maritime history of Castlehaven:

Brendan O'Neill and *Wally O'Neill* for their knowledge of fishing boats;

Joy and *David Woosnam* on the Silver Fleet;

Dan Somerville on Tom the Merchant;

Colette O'Sullivan for correcting my spellings of words in Irish;

Peter Somerville-Large for his expert advice and help with the manuscript, and for kindly writing the foreword;

Vanessa Turner who kindly proofread the manuscript;

Lisa Boland for typing the manuscript;

Lady Coghill for permission to reproduce the photographs taken by Egerton and Joscelyn Coghill;

My late father, *Paul Chavasse*, who passed on to me his great knowledge of Castlehaven's history;

And finally, *Patricia*, for her forbearance and encouragement while I was writing. To her, I dedicate this book.

Castlehaven

On the south coast of Ireland, in the county of Cork, between Glandore to the east and Baltimore to the west, there is an inlet of the sea called Castlehaven. This inlet, or harbour, runs from the south-west to the north-east. It is very sheltered, except from the south and south-east, since the harbour mouth, of about two cables wide, faces in that direction. On each side of the entrance is located an island: Skiddy to the east and Horse Island to the west, with Black Rock about a cable to the south of that island. From Horse Island to the League – a naturally formed spit of land at the eastern end of the harbour – is one nautical mile. The widest part of the harbour is about 700 yards, and the narrowest about one cable, or 200 yards.

Castlehaven acquired its name from the two castles built around 1584 at either end of the harbour. At the eastern end of the harbour, O'Dovovan Mór built his castle – now called Raheen Castle. At the other end, by the old village of St Barrahane, O'Driscoll Mór, the Chief of Collymore, had built his own castle, subsequently called Castlehaven Castle. In the reign of Queen Elizabeth I, they were bombarded by her ships of the Navy Royal – as it was then known – because Sir Fineen O'Driscoll, with the help of the Spaniards, held Castlehaven against her ships.

Raheen Castle is still standing, though the roof of the main hall has fallen in, leaving only its chevron on the tower wall. The seaward-facing wall is pock-marked and bruised by the cannon-balls of Elizabeth's ships.

As for Castlehaven Castle – it suddenly decided it could no longer stand, its power and purpose past and gone, and it died without ceremony on the morning of 25 February 1926, sinking down upon its foundations with a rumbling roar.

facing page
This photograph was taken c. 1895 by Sir Joscelyn Coghill, a founder member of the Royal Hibernian Photographic Society. In the foreground, Hildegarde Coghill, in Glen Barahane garden, contemplates the French fishing boats. In search of mackerel and herring, they came mostly from Fecamp.

The Battle of Castlehaven 1601

For some years, the agents in Spain of O'Neill and O'Donnell had been urging the Spanish to invade Ireland. In the spring of 1601, the Roman Catholic Archbishop of Dublin, a Spaniard named Mates de Oviedo, arrived back in Spain. He also supported the call to invade, as did Aodh Budhe, the chief Irish agent in Spain, together with several others, notably some Irish friars working in that country.

As it happened, a large army was being assembled in Spain to enforce certain claims in Flanders, and King Philip was persuaded to make this army ready for invading Ireland. A fleet of some fifty ships was assembled in Cadiz, together with 4,000 soldiers, their guns and ordnance. However, about half of the warships had to be diverted to escort a valuable convoy of transports coming from the West Indies. This delayed the fleet, and it finally set sail from Lisbon with twenty-seven ships under the command of Don Diego de Brochero in his flagship *San Pedro*. Owing to bad weather and news of an English squadron in the offing, only about half the fleet reached Kinsale, where the soldiers landed unopposed and captured the town.

On 3 December, a report reached the English that a Spanish squadron of six ships, under the command of Vice-admiral Pedro de Zubiar – de Brochero's second-in-command – had arrived in Castlehaven. As Zubiar approached Castlehaven, he saw a boat pulling out of the harbour but did not know if she contained 'los Hereticos' or their supporters. To his relief, he learned that she was manned by four O'Driscoll brothers – Donagh, Dermot, Cornelius and Darius – who were in possession of St Barrahane's Castle close to the village and just within the entrance to the harbour. Through the medium of Latin, the O'Driscoll brothers communicated with a priest on board and, having identified themselves, navigated the squadron into the harbour to a comfortable anchorage under the castle.

Realising the English would react when they heard the news that Zubiar was in Castlehaven, the Spaniards brought in their five transports and beached them on the strand below the castle. The stores were secured and

facing page
Raheen Castle.

| 11

their guns brought up to and mounted on Battery Point, which overlooks the entrance of the harbour. There was, however, room for no more than four boats on the strand, so they sent the fifth, a flyboat, up harbour to be out of harm's way. They were not a moment too soon, for when Admiral Sir Richard Leveson – who was in Kinsale Harbour – heard the news that Zubiar was in Castlehaven, he immediately set sail and proceeded there with his flagship, *Warspite*, together with *Defiance*, *Swiftsure*, *Crane* and a caravel named *Merlin*. As soon as he reached Castlehaven, he sent *Merlin* ahead to take soundings at the entrance to see if there was enough water for entering. Leveson then lead his ships into the harbour and sank Zubiar's flagship, *Leon de Oro*, which lay at anchor off the strand. *Warspite* then ran aground, possibly in Castlehaven Haul, and was bombarded by the Spanish guns mounted on Battery Point. Fortunately for Leveson, the wind, which had been south-east, veered to the south-west, and he was able to claw his way out of the harbour and sail, battered and bruised, with the rest of his squadron back to Kinsale.

Unfortunately, history does not relate what part in the action the rest of his squadron had taken. Leveson did not cover himself in glory. Apart from sinking *Leon de Oro*, Leveson should have smashed or set fire to all transports on the strand and sunk or captured the fly-boat. All these ships eventually found their way back to Spain. *Warspite*, though badly damaged, did not have to go into dock, and was soon repaired and ready for further action if required.

The sailors killed aboard *Leon de Oro* were buried in a field above Reen Point. Later, the captain of the ship was disinterred and his body sent back to Spain for burial. The others lie in peace overlooking the sea.

The battle at Castlehaven had an influence on the subsequent siege at Kinsale and on the Irish forces supporting the Spanish, though O'Sullivan Beare – alone among the Irish leaders – was not daunted by the sudden downfall of their forces and fortunes. He wrote to Don Juan de Aguila – the Spanish land commander-in-chief – urging him not to lose courage or surrender Kinsale. But it was too late. Aguila decided not to risk further bombardment and loss of life, and he negotiated with Mountjoy, offering surrender of the town if allowed to march out with honours of war. Mountjoy accepted, and the Spanish soldiers boarded their ships with their weapons and sailed back to Spain.

The revenge of the English on the Irish who had supported the Spaniards was swift and terrible. In Dursey Island alone, over 300 men, women and children were massacred. Huge areas of corn around Bantry were burned, and it was hoped by the English authorities that this would cause famine. It did. The same revenge was meted out to the 'rebels' in Tyrone and Antrim as had befallen those in Cork. Pacenta Hibernia had been achieved.

The Silver Fleet

I n the early 1600s, the Spanish government was sending transports to the Spanish Main, where soldiers went as far south as Peru, plundering gold, silver and precious stones. However, during one expedition in 1628, 'los conquistadores' – as the Spanish soldiers had become known – received orders to bring back only silver. This silver was loaded into a collection of their ships, which became known as the Silver Fleet, and set sail for Spain. *En route*, they ran into a strong easterly gale in mid-Atlantic which blew the fleet back to the area of the Florida Keys, where they met a powerful Dutch squadron under the command of Admiral Piet Heyn. At that time, Holland was at war with Spain, and a bitter battle was fought which ended in all the Spanish transports being captured. Prize crews were put on board the captured transports and, under the command of Lieutenant Peter Franzy, they sailed for Holland. However, as they approached the south-west of Ireland, they ran into a south-westerly gale. One of the transports, *Santa Anna Maria* – thought to have been in the Spanish Armada forty years earlier – may

have been a straggler or was blown off course, and was washed ashore onto Reen Point at the entrance to Castlehaven, where she became a total wreck. She might have been seeking shelter in Castlehaven, or it is possible she went onto the rocks of Black Rock or Skiddy.

Shortly after the wrecking, a man called Johansson – a merchant from Baltimore – dived on the wreck in a primitive sort of diving bell. Johansson found a number of artefacts, including most, if not all, the silver. In 1968, Sid and David Woosnam dived on the wreck. A local farmer who owned the land by Reen Point had pointed out the site of the wreck. They found a pewter board, two rusted iron cannon and two very fine bronze cannon about 12 feet long, with the coat of arms of King Philip II of Spain on their breeches. As Ireland was neutral at the time of the shipwreck, the contents raised by Sid and David Woosnam have had to be returned to Spain.

It is not known if the sailors who were drowned in the wreck were buried alongside those of *Leon de Oro*.

Fishing Boats

From time immemorial, men fished the harbour and its approaches for mackerel, pollack, cod, herring and shellfish. Originally, they lived with their families in the small village of St Barrahane – named after a local saint – which was situated at the north-western end of the harbour and under the protection of a branch of the O'Driscoll sept, which owned the castle that overlooked the village and its church. It was to the village of St Barrahane that these fishermen brought their catches, where it was eaten by their families or sold to people living inland from the coast.

Fish were caught in crude nets or with lines made from strong grasses, reeds or willow. There were never any currachs in Cork but it possible that the earliest boats were constructed in much the same way as currachs, with skins stretched over a wooden frame and oiled to keep water out.

As the village faced south, it was very exposed to weather from that quarter, and many a boat must have been wrecked during a southerly gale, when they were caught on the lee shore. These primitive and frail craft could not stay at sea or even just outside the harbour if it came on to blow. If it did, they would have to high-tail quickly back to the shelter of the harbour. In the late 1600s, it was decided to move the village – lock, stock and barrel – to the place where Castletownshend stands today. This gives a more sheltered position. It must have been quite an undertaking. The name was changed to Castletownshend by the Townsend family, who had been given land in the area by Oliver Cromwell. Access to the harbour from the new village was different to that of today. A quay – now called the Western Quay – was built at the bottom of the then village hill. Boats came alongside this quay for discharging their catch of fish and for repairs, bottom-scrubbing and general maintenance.

Prior to the 1880s, the fishing boats based in Castlehaven were small, heavy to handle and open to the elements. Furthermore, they were not good sea-boats; in reasonably calm conditions, they could fish to within about ten miles of the harbour. They were propelled by oars using thole-pins instead of crutches; these oars

facing page
Lobsterboat moored off Seafield, c. 1930. These boats, known as towelsail yawls, sailed from Heir Island and the Calf islands in Roaringwater Bay.
over
Fishing boats at Fish Quay, c. 1865–80.

were long and heavy with a narrow blade. They did, however, have an advantage in that they could be used as a prop for an awning over the centre part of the boat so the crew could keep relatively warm, dry and sheltered when they had a fire for cooking. This awning was usually one of the sails, which was hoisted when the wind was abaft the beam.

Over the years, fishing boats became larger and very much more seaworthy and, by the 1890s, many in Castlehaven were around 70 feet and known as 'netters', as they caught fish – mainly mackerel or herring – in large nets. Many of these boats had long bowsprits which gave them a classical look. Most had two masts and some were square-rigged on their main while others had a fore-and-aft rig. The mizzen had a spanker which was usually kept hoisted both at sea and while at anchor. It helped to keep the boat steady in a rough sea and her

French fishing boats, Castlehaven Harbour, c. 1865–80.

head to wind while at anchor. They relied on their sails most of the time, though some of them had a small steam engine that was fired by coal. This engine did not have much power and could only push the boats, in calm conditions, at about 3–4 knots. They must have looked a fine sight beating to windward with all their sails set when going to sea, and later when running back to their moorings with a flock of gulls following in their wake, devouring the fish guts that the crew threw over the side. They had around twelve to fourteen members of crew, all of whom were employed for sailing the boat, steering with the large tiller and tending to the net while fishing. In those days, of course, there were no winches for pulling in the net, which must have been extremely heavy, especially when full of fish. However, most had a capstan to help haul the net. This was worked by hand using capstan-bars placed into holes on the head of the

capstan, and a man walked round pushing his bar. The capstan was not only used for hauling in the nets but also for swaying spars up the masts and lifting heavy objects. The ropes used in these boats were sisal, which were tarred to keep them from rotting, but this made them stiff and awkward to use. The nets were cotton which had been dipped overnight in a bark dye from South Africa.

Gradually, over the years, these large fishing boats gave way to slightly smaller and more economical and efficient craft, and by the 1920s and 1930s, trawling, which was taking over from netting, became popular, as the trawls brought in a variety of fish for which there was always a good price in the markets. The seabed in Scullane Bay, Castlehaven Harbour entrance and to the south of High Island were suitable places for trawling, as they had sandy bottoms. Two of the leading marks that the trawlers used were Nelson's Arch and the Fir, a strange vertical piece of rock that sticks up in a cleft on High Island.

In the 1920s and 1930s, lobsterboats became popular. They were around 20 feet with a mast and a heavy sail made of canvas. They sometimes had a foresail which, like many of the earlier boats, could be used as an awning. One of the larger fishing boats of that period was the *Swan*, which had a small Kelvin paraffin engine and was used for trawling. Her bones are lying just beyond the Corrigeen, where part of her keel can still be seen at low tide. There were a number of open 20-foot boats that had sails, and these continued to be fished until the outbreak of the Second World War. One of them, when returning from mackerel fishing near Low Island, was hit by a vicious squall which capsized her. She sank with the tragic loss of all hands.

Fishing boat moored off Reen Pier, c. 1920.

When the weather was fair, especially in June and July, mammals and big fish were seen by crews of fishing boats. Whales, basking sharks, porpoises and sun-fish were all seen not far from Castlehaven. Seals were not liked by fishermen as when they pursued mackerel, they were prone to becoming entangled in nets and tore them. Sometimes, turtles were caught in a net; these were released if not too entangled.

It was at the end of the nineteenth century that European countries like France and Spain heard that there was a big fishing potential of herring near the south and south-west coast of Ireland and, consequently, huge fleets of French and Spanish fishing boats came and fished off the coast. Many called into Castletownshend where they discharged their catches for the Continent. In those days, there were no freezer compartments in the holds of fishing boats. Scores of women were employed gutting and cleaning fish on the quay and packing them into boxes for transport to Cork. These foreign boats continued to fish off the Cork coast and land their catches in Castletownshend and other south-coast ports until the 1920s. On the League, fish were salted and packed in barrels which were placed in Sheehy's store behind Reen Pier, from where they were taken to Cork.

Over the following years, the size and design of fishing boats changed. The new ones, while still made of timber, had better and stronger equipment. Ropes and nets began to be made from synthetic fibre, and most had winches and oil-fired engines which were not only more reliable than the old coal-fired or kerosene engines but also considerably increased the boat's range. They also had echo and depth-sounders, radios, refrigeration plants and radar. Some of the smaller boats concentrated on lobster and crab fishing while others fished for shrimp, and their pots – originally made from

reeds or willow – were now made of plastic. Some of the men who owned boats of 25–30 feet fished for salmon, which was becoming popular. The season for catching salmon is very short; it starts at the beginning of June and ends on the last day of July, and lasts for four days each week. The fish run from east to west and are caught in a drift-net with an unmoored buoy at one end and a boat on the other, which occasionally goes ahead in order to keep the net taut. The net is about a quarter of a mile long and 10 feet deep, and is hauled every two hours.

From the 1980s to the present, trawlers – made of steel – have become larger and much more sophisticated. Unfortunately, there is no record of most of the names of the old fishing boats. *Carbery Lass* and *Bonny Lass* were both converted ship's lifeboats, and it is believed that the former was from the *Lusitania*. They were found washed up somewhere along the coast and were later given a wheelhouse, and 13–15h.p. engines were installed. Their owners used them to fish for eel, with long lines baited with hooks. All these boats have now gone – some just rotted away; others, like the *Swan*, stripped of their gear and fittings, were towed up beyond the League to their final resting places in the mud or on a rock under an overhanging tree. Their weed-covered timbers can still be seen sticking up through the mud at low tide, like the ribs of some prehistoric animal. Now there are only five inshore boats left in Castlehaven; they are *Lough Croin*, *Tino Cnuna*, *Ann Caroline*, *Ireland Lass* and *Meave Eileen*. Most are used for salmon fishing during the season, but for the rest of the year, they fish for white fish, lobster, crab, shrimp and scallops. Only one trawler – the *Carrick Brac* – brings her catch to Reen Pier; all the others go to Union Hall where there is a modern pier, ice-plant and fish-processing plant.

facing page
Fish Quay,
c. 1865–80.

Mahony's Boat-Building Store

In the 1830s, a store for grain was built on the quay at the bottom of the village hill (this quay was not the Fish Quay of today, but the one to the west, which was built when the village of St Barrahane moved from Castlehaven). This store has an archway under it which fills with water at high tide and into which a barge was floated. A trapdoor opened in the roof of the arch to allow sacks of grain to be lowered into the barge. When loaded, the barge was taken out to a lighter that was moored off the quay, and the sacks of grain transferred into her. When full, the lighter was floated and poled – on a flood tide – to the mill at Rineen from where the grain was taken by cart to Cork.

In the 1840s, this grain store was bought by Martin Mahony, who turned it into a boat store and where he designed and built boats. Many of Martin's sons, grandsons and nephews served their apprenticeships in this building before they moved onto boat and ship-building in Cork, Dublin and England.

Designing a sailing boat is an art rather than a science. Without any knowledge of hydrodynamics or many of the natural laws that today are accepted as commonplace, a boat designer like Martin knew from experience that a fat and squat hull would sail slower and not go to windward so well as a slim one. A slim hull would go to windward better but would heel more in a given wind. Martin and his sons knew about this and they adapted their drawings and models to make boats that would both go well to windward and not heel too much. All the boats they built encompassed these two principles. First, they drew the sections of boats on paper and laid them out on the floor of the boathouse loft, just as a dressmaker might. These drawings were then transferred to thin wood, and the wooden patterns were nailed to the timber that was to be shaped. It was important to find the best piece of timber for the stem-piece. This was usually oak and, with luck, was the correct shape; more often than not, it had to be bent into the desired curve by putting it into a vat of boiling water until it became pliable enough to bend. The ribs were also made of oak, and they too had to be boiled and bent to the correct curve. Each rib had a slightly different curve from the next one, so it was a test of the builder's skill. These ribs were then fitted to the keel, an extension of the stem; in larger boats, the keelson was fitted running parallel to the keel and above it. The transom for rudder was fitted, to which the pintle and gudgeon were later attached. The boat now stood like a skeleton, and work started on the planking, and later the caulking between the planks – with oakum or lengths of old rope – in order to prevent the ingress of water into the boat.

Some boats were carvel-built, meaning the planks touched each other without overlapping, and this made for a smooth hull. Others were clinker-built – their planks overlapped, somewhat like a clapboard house. This made a heavier hull, but was much stronger. When all this work was complete, the decking was added, and the hull, both inside and out, was painted with a priming coat and a couple of finishing coats. And so the boat was at last ready for launching. Even after launching, there was still a lot to do. The mast had to be stepped and the rigging set up, the halyards had to be rove and the sails bent on. She also had to be ballasted and a mass of other items added before she was ready for sea.

While over the years the Mahonys designed and built some beautiful boats, there was one class of boat that was not totally Mahony-designed. These sailing boats became know as the 'Ette' class for which Castletownshend has become renowned. They are about 16 feet overall, with a beam of about 5 feet 9 inches. Around their centre-plate casing are ten pigs of lead for ballast, each weighing 20 pounds. Their clinker-built hulls are half-decked and they have a short bowsprit. The rig is standing lug (or gunter), with the gaff set hard against the mast. The main is quite large and the jib is small, with the result that when sailing off the wind in a rough sea and a fresh wind, it could be quite exciting, as broaching-to was a possibility. However, apart from that, they are good sea-boats, which is a requirement outside the harbour.

Their story began some time in the early 1930s, when an attractive-looking craft sailed into Castlehaven. Though she was a good bit longer than the subsequent Ettes, she possessed their general outline, and her appearance, as she lay at anchor, appealed to Jerh and Jim Mahony. When her owner had gone up the village hill to Mary Ann's bar, the two men went on board and measured her up: hull, spars and sails. Later, they produced plans for an Ette – a scaled-down version of the boat they had measured. In the trade, to scale down a boat and produce a craft that could sail well was looked upon as being a remarkable achievement. There was, at this time, a locally owned boat, not built in Castletownshend and not too dissimilar to the Ettes, except she carried no ballast (her centre-plate was large and heavy). Her name was *Suzette*, and it was she who gave the new boats their Ette name. Built in 1897, she was already old when the Ettes were built. She is still about, but will need a lot of repair and attention to get her seaworthy and sailing again.

The sounds of the saw and hammer were finally stilled following Jim's death in 1968, having been almost constant since 1840. For some years, the building lay a ruin. The roof had fallen in, and the wind and rain were gradually spoiling what was a fine old boat-house. However, in 1975, it was bought by Bayard and Margaret Warren, an American couple who were keen on boats and owned a small yacht called *Lily*. They had the building repaired and, following Bayard's death, it was used for artistic exhibitions and lectures, thereby giving much pleasure to the people of Castletownshend and from further afield.

The Coastguard
Station

In 1840, the British Admiralty leased about an acre of land from the Somerville family on the north side of the harbour, where it is at its most narrow. The property included all the land above mean high tide, plus the strand above mean high tide. On this acre, in 1841, they built the first coastguard station in Ireland. A two-storey building housed the coastguard men and their families, while a separate building housed

Coastguard station boat-house, c. 1930.

the rocket machine. In an emergency, this device was used to fire, by rocket, a line to a stricken vessel by which the crew was pulled ashore to safety.

There was also a fine stone-built boat-house made on the same lines as the station, which housed the lifeboat – a cutter. This boat was 25 feet long and clinker-built. When rowed, eight men – two on each thwart – pulled her. When sailing, she had two masts with a dipping lug on the fore and a standing lug on the main. This type of rig gave way in the twentieth century to the 32-foot cutter which had a different rig. The coxswain of the cutter lived with his family in a building that was attached to the south side of the boat-house. Unfortunately, there is no record as to whether this life-boat ever rescued or attempted to rescue anyone.

During the War of Independence, this coastguard station, like most of the others around Ireland, was burnt down by the IRA. It lay a ruin until the early 1950s, when the land was bought from the government and the shell of the old station made into a dwelling house, which later was called 'The Rocket House'. There is a bench-mark close to the flagstaff of The Rocket House that was emplaced by the Ordnance Survey in March 1841 and was used in connection with tide observations at Castletownshend in 1842. Castle-townshend was the first of twenty-two stations around the coast at which observations were taken to determine the datum to be used for height data on Ordnance Survey maps.

Castlehaven Hydrographic Survey

Before 1846, the harbour of Castlehaven had never been surveyed, so the Admiral Superintendent in charge of all the coastguard stations around Ireland informed their lordships at the Admiralty about this matter. In 1846, five years after the coastguard station in Castletownshend had been built, HMS *Hecla*, commanded by Commander J. Wolfe, was given orders to survey the harbour, its approaches and other areas along the south Cork coast. The survey of the harbour was carried out by *Hecla*'s boats, with Lieutenant Church in charge.

In those days, before echo-sounders, surveying a seabed was carried out by hand with a lead and line. A seaman was given an apron of sword-matting, with a canvas flap, to keep his clothes dry. When sounding from a ship's boat, he had a $2^1/_2$-pound line about 12 fathoms long marked in feet up to 4 fathoms, and after that in single fathoms. On the end of the line was a 7-pound lead weight in a leg-o'-mutton shape, with a hollow in the bottom which was filled with tallow. The nature of the seabed could be seen from the imprint in the tallow – be it sand, gravel, mud, stones or rock. The leadsman, standing in the bow of the boat, looped the line in his left hand with a bight in his right, and he threw the lead and line ahead of the boat. When the boat had moved ahead and the line was vertical, the leadsman called out the depth, which was recorded in a book. Bearings were, of course, taken on the exact spot of the recorded depth. As the boat was propelled by other seamen pulling on oars, the whole operation must have been very laborious and enormously time-consuming, especially when it is considered that over eighty soundings were taken and recorded between Horse Island and Rineen Mill.

'Tom the Merchant' & Other Stories

In 1755, Thomas Somerville came to Castle-townshend from Scotland, and in 1759 married Mary, the daughter of Philip Townsend, thus acquiring the land where Drishane (in Irish, 'the Place of Brambles') now stands. He and Mary had eleven children.

Thomas – who later became know as 'Tom the Merchant' – built a small fleet of ships which he based in Castlehaven. The voyages of his trading ships were advertised in *Hibernia* magazine: 'The good Ship . . . of 250 tons burthen will sail from Castlehaven to . . . on . . .' Trading mainly in the West Indies, he himself made several voyages to that area and also to Newfoundland, carrying big consignments of butter and salted provisions, and bringing home to Castlehaven cargoes of rum, sugar and wine. While awaiting further transport, these goods were stored in the store-house that he built on Western Quay.

The captains of his ships complained that it was difficult to see the entrance to Castlehaven when their ships approached from the sea, so he built a tower on Horse Island as a day-mark – the tower still stands. His ships also brought the limestone window-sills from Cork which are to this day in Drishane House.

Dutchman's Cove

It was during the time of Tom the Merchant that a southerly gale forced a small Dutch transport to be driven ashore on the north side of the harbour, opposite the entrance. She was carrying a cargo of timber, and much of this timber was used for the roof trusses and beams in Drishane. The place of the wreck became known as Dutchman's Cove.

Nelson's Arch

In late October 1805, a naval schooner entered Castlehaven. She was HMS *Pickle*, commanded by Lieutenant Lapengtiere – an Englishman, though undoubtedly of French extraction – who was bringing to the Admiralty in London dispatches of the Battle of Trafalgar of 21 October and news of the death of Vice-admiral Lord Nelson. After a stormy passage, *Pickle* called in at

Castlehaven to take on water before proceeding to Plymouth. So the people of Castletownshend learned about the battle and of the death of Lord Nelson before the English government. To commemorate the event, an arch – called Nelson's Arch – was built to the north-east of Castlehaven and overlooking the harbour and its approaches. For many years, this arch was used by fishermen as a mark for trawling. It was demolished by republicans during the civil war in 1922, later rebuilt, and again demolished by the IRA in 1971. Today, there is just a small pile of stones.

Naval Ships in Castlehaven

During the First World War, a flotilla of Royal Navy minesweepers was stationed at Haulbowline, in order to keep the harbours and approaches of Cork and Castletownbere clear of mines. This flotilla sometimes called at Castlehaven and anchored opposite Dutchman's Cove, where there are around 4 fathoms of water and plenty of room for those ships to swing. In the 1920s, destroyers and motor launches sometimes anchored in the harbour. In 1917, the crew of the motor launch, ML 320, found a ladder drifting in the sea not far from Castlehaven. They gave this ladder to St Barrahane's Church, so people could climb up into the belfry.

Seaplanes also landed in Castlehaven in the 1920s. They usually anchored near the League – which was reasonably sheltered – and their crew paddled themselves ashore in a small, canvas dinghy. These days, patrol ships of the Irish Naval Service anchor off Bilawn, where they usually spend the night in order to give their crews a breather from fishery-protection duties and chasing drug-runners. Tenders of Irish Lights also occasionally visit Castlehaven – and sometimes spend a night at anchor – when on their annual inspection of buoys and lighthouses around the coast of Ireland.

Faill Dick

A very small strand, called Faill Dick, is situated between Castlehaven Strand and Poul Girm, where the shingle is particularly fine and even. Those requiring gravel for a drive or garden path obtained it from there. A barge was towed to the strand, where it was run aground at half-tide. Men then loaded the barge with gravel before floating off at the next high tide, accompanied by much pushing and shoving. The barge was towed slowly back to the quay at Castletownshend, where the shingle was loaded into sacks, put into a cart and pulled by horse up to the house from where it had been ordered.

In the early 1920s, a load of this gravel was taken to Glen Barrahane, where it was spread on the avenue. A few days later, someone who was walking down the avenue spotted a ring in the gravel. It featured a diamond stone surrounded by small rubies, and later became known as the 'Lusitania Ring'. The liner *Lusitania*, *en route* from America to England, had been sunk off the Old Head of Kinsale in 1915, so it was possible that this ring was brought by currents from the wreck and finally washed ashore on Faill Dick. This ring was left to my daughter, Kate, by her grandmother. Unfortunately, history does not relate who Faill Dick was or why the strand is called by that name.

Colliers in Castlehaven

Ever since coal was used in domestic houses and in old fishing boats, it was imported to Castletownshend by colliers from ports in south Wales or Bristol. These colliers discharged the coal onto the Fish Quay, where it was put into sacks, loaded into horse-drawn carts and pulled up the village hill to different houses. One of the last colliers to deliver coal to Castletownshend – in 1924 – was the *Kathleen and May*, a three-masted vessel with a fore-and-aft rig.

facing page top
HMS Wolfhound, *a Royal Navy destroyer (launched 1918, decommissioned 1948), in Castlehaven in the early part of the twentieth century;*

centre, left
Seaplane moored by the League, c. 1925;

centre, right
ML 259 moored by Corrigeen, c. 1917;

bottom
Minesweepers in Castlehaven, c. 1915.

Some Yachts of Castlehaven

U p till the end of the eighteenth century, there was no pleasure boating in West Cork. Glandore had the first pleasure boats, around the turn of that century, when some men sailed down from Cork. These men may have gone further west and called in at Castlehaven, though there is no record of them having done so. In the 1890s, there were a number of pleasure boats in Castlehaven. These were around 20 feet overall and had long bowsprits and were either rigged as topsail cutters or yawls. Although they had main booms, their mainsails were loose-footed. We know the names of three of these boats: *Gyneth*, *Thea* and *Haidee*.

Pleasure boating in Castlehaven was largely dominated by four Anglo-Irish families who lived in Castletownshend from around 1850 to the start of the Second World War. They lived in large houses whose gardens ran into each other, and owned punts, dinghies and small yachts in which they raced against each other under the umbrella of the South Cork Sailing Club, which they had founded shortly after the start of the

twentieth century. They also went on picnics together to the various strands and islands in and around Castlehaven. By the end of the war, most of these families had either left Castletownshend or had died out. Their boats lingered on for a few more years until they became too old or too dangerous to take to sea, and they were either sold or broken up, as will be told later.

One of the first larger yachts from Castlehaven was *Ierne*. She was 65 feet overall and built on the Clyde in 1854, where she was rigged as a schooner with a flying jib, fore-staysail, fore and mainsails (both of which were loose-footed) and a topsail set above the main. Her fine carvel-built hull had a long sheer leading up to her bowsprit. Her deck was teak and she was steered by an immense tiller made of mahogany. A Turk's head was carved at the forward end, on one side of which was the owner's family crest. Slightly back from the Turk's head was a brass collar around which was bent a half-hitch of rope that was held by the helmsman in heavy weather. In 1908, her masts were removed and for many years she lay at her moorings in Castlehaven as a houseboat with

facing page
Castlehaven, by
Neville Swinchat.

a large and hideous 'dog-house' on her deck – a sad and forlorn sight after her previous grandeur. Unfortunately, she broke her moorings in a storm in 1917 and was washed ashore and wrecked.

Around the start of the 1900s, a number of families in Castletownshend bought small yachts; these were more modern than those that were around in Castlehaven in the previous century. Some of these yachts were used solely for trawling, but most of them were used for pleasure and racing in regattas, not only in Castlehaven but also at Glandore, Baltimore, Schull and Sherkin.

The oldest of these boats was *Violet*, built in 1880. She was a sloop with a loose-footed main and a topsail, and was very slow. She was carvel-built and had a deep keel made of wood, so bits and pieces of iron were placed in her bilges as ballast. She was used only for trawling.

Bat was designed and built by the Mahonys in 1898. She was a fine cutter made of mahogany with a teak deck. Her stem was straight and she had a long, heavy keel and a long counter. The author can remember being seasick in her when sailing through Stag's Sound in the late 1940s, shortly before she was sold.

Remora was different from all the other yachts in Castlehaven in that her hull was clinker-built and, although she had a gaff above her main, there was no topsail as the peak halyard brought the gaff close to the mast. She was built in Oban in 1895; after winning a number of races on the Clyde, she was sold and later sailed to Castlehaven. She had a short bowsprit and a sawn-off counter and her length at the waterline was 22 feet 6 inches with a beam of 5 foot 9 inches. Weighing 2 tons in total, more than half of this weight was in her large lead keel, which drew 4 feet. Both her main and jib,

Remora *(left) and* Guillimot *in Castlehaven Harbour.*

measuring in total 393 square feet, were made by Ratsey and Lapthorn in 1905, who also made her balloon jib of cotton-silk and her storm jib of canvas. Having a low freeboard, she was inclined to be very wet when going to windward in any sea. Her end sadly came in 1949 when she was fifty-four years old. She had been sold to a man in Howth and was sunk in a gale when a fishing boat came alongside and crushed her against the pier.

Guillimot was built around 1900 as a carvel-built topsail sloop of 24 feet. Like *Remora*, she was half-decked and had a well for the crew. She also had a short bowsprit. When she was sold to an Aer Lingus pilot in 1950, she left Castlehaven. She was seen a few years later on a cradle near Cork Airport.

Thea I was a half-decked, 22-foot, topsail cutter. Like many other yachts of her generation, she had a long bowsprit and a long, deep keel. In her latter years,

she took tourists fishing, until she became too old and dangerous to go to sea.

Thea II was almost a copy of *Guillimot*. She was designed and built by Jerh Mahony and was the largest yacht the Mahonys had ever built, being 27 feet overall.

Spray was a carvel-built, topsail sloop and – like many of the others – had a straight stem and a long, heavy keel. Like *Violet*, she was very slow and was used for trawling.

Dea was the smallest of these yachts, being only 18 feet. She was built in Cork in 1902 and was a sloop with a topsail.

Valeta was built in the 1920s and was 22 feet overall. She, too, was carvel-built and was a sloop, but was never properly balanced as she had a very heavy weather helm, so was liable to fly up into the wind unless a firm hand was on her tiller.

left to right
Bat, Guillimot *and* Remora *in Castlehaven, c. 1930.*

There were other boats, such as *Mab*, which were never raced and seldom, if ever, ventured out of the harbour. There was also *Stag*, which was taken to Haulbowline in the 1920s by the captain in charge of the naval base. And there was *Leda*, which was like a small yacht of about 16 feet. She had very light fittings and bamboo spars.

None of these boats had an engine, so to propel them in light airs or in times of danger, they carried a single sweep, or very long oar. As part of their rigging, they all had runners. Their sails were made of cotton or cotton-duck and their storm jibs were made of canvas. One disadvantage of cotton sails was that they were inclined to shrink into odd shapes if they were not properly stretched when new. Another disadvantage was if they got wet with rain or especially saltwater and were put into a sail-cover, they very quickly became covered in mildew.

None of these boats had winches. Their main sheets were rove through wooden blocks on the end of their boom, but their jib sheets were pulled in by brute force and belayed onto a cleat. Ropes in those days were not synthetic but hemp, manila, sisal or occasionally Egyptian cotton. Manila was usually used for the sheets and hemp for halyards. Likejackets were seldom, if ever, worn. They were bulky and uncomfortable and were made of kapok or cork. Fortunately, there is no record of any fatality. There were no such luxuries as guard-rails, stainless-steel shrouds or stays, bottle-screws, Tufnal or stainless-steel blocks, jam cleats, synthetic rope that did not kink or rot, galleys, roller jibs, easy-reefing mainsails or oilskins that do not stick together after storage.

Everyone who owned a boat in Castlehaven kept her on a standing mooring; to reach them, they had rowing boats – or punts, as they are called locally – on running moorings. Many of these punts had outboard engines which meant they could take people on picnics without too much effort on the part of the owner.

In their time, they filled their purpose and gave much pleasure to a lot of people. They are now history, and their place has been taken by fibreglass boats such as Wayfarers, Toppers, Mirrors, Lazers and Day-boats, all of which have their merits and advantages; but they do not have the same 'feel' as wooden boats. Though the old boats were hard work – especially if it was blowing – they were nevertheless most enjoyable to sail.

The Centreboard Class

I n Castlehaven, the other class of boat sailed for pleasure and raced was known as the centreboard class. These clinker-built boats were built around 1890. Originally, they were glorified punts and very heavy. Their usual length was 14 feet, except *Bantam*, which was 15 feet, and *Curlew*, a little over 13 feet.

They were rigged as dinghies around 1900, when they were given a centre-plate and casing. A thick, wooden mast, with no shrouds, was stepped through a thwart about 2 feet abaft the stem. At first, they had no jib, but later, a short bowsprit was added, and a small jib improved their sailing qualities. They were all rigged with a standing lug (or gunter), and the main boom stuck well out over the stern. Around the early 1930s, *Ierne* was re-rigged with a tall mast and given a Bermuda rig – her owner thought it would make her faster and point better; she certainly pointed better, but she was no faster. For ballast, all the class had eight 20-pound pigs of lead arranged round their centre-plate casing, and – having no decking – if they capsized, they sank. Buoyancy tanks took up too much space, it seems. *Woodcock* had a

rounded stern. *Bantam* was built in Castlehaven by Mahony Bros. All the others were bought in Cork or on the east coast. Apart from the aforementioned *Bantam*, *Ierne*, *Curlew* and *Woodcock*, there was *Wild Goose*, *Gamecock*, *Banshee* and *Dabchick*.

When sailing these boats, there could be exciting moments. Although by modern standards they were not fast, they were prone – when running before a fresh wind – to bury their bows, so it was sensible to bring one's crew as far aft as possible; otherwise, they could be driven under and swamped – then they would sink. Having no kicking-strap, their boom was inclined to lift while running, so there was always a danger of a Chinese gybe. Like the yachts, these boats all had cotton sails so the same problems occurred with these sails when they became wet or damp.

Both the yachts and dinghies died out in the late 1940s and early 1950s. They were all very old and their upkeep and maintenance were crippling. As most of them were laid up during the war, they became rotten and leaked like sieves.

The Ette Class

The class of boat that succeeded the yachts and the centreboard class was the Ettes. The story of how they came about has already been told. As they carried a lot of ballast round their centreboard casings, they sank if they capsized, prompting some of their owners to install buoyancy tanks. However, these tanks took up a lot of space below and so were not very successful.

The first Ette to be built was *Alouette*, in 1932. Her deck was all wood with a convex construction. After rotting for many years, she was restored in Dungarvan and is once again being sailed and raced in Castlehaven. *Avocet* was the only Ette to be fitted with a Bermuda rig, and in spite of being 16 feet 6 inches long, she was not a successful boat. *Coquette* was built in 1936, and to make her higher out of the water, she was given an extra plank, or strake. She is still being sailed and raced in Castlehaven. *Pirouette* was a heavy boat – her deck was of wooden planks which may have accounted for this rather excessive weight. *Jeanette* was built in 1950 and, after a few seasons' racing, was wrecked during a storm in 1986.

Mignonette was built in 1951 and unfortunately fell to pieces, as she was stored in the open. *Sagette* was built in 1952. Unfortunately, she was not a good boat and changed owners three times. *Lilybet*, built in 1953, was only sailed in races but never won. *Marianette* was built in 1954; despite her hull being 6 inches longer than any of the others, she was a slow boat. *Ninette* was built in 1955 – Jim Mahony said she was the best boat he had built. Her hull and spars were lighter than the other Ettes, helping to make her a fast boat. Although she was badly damaged during a storm in 1961, she was repaired extremely well and is still being sailed. *Colette*, built in 1958, was the first of the class to have terelene sails; a good sea-boat, she was also fast. *Rosette*, built in 1960, had one less plank than the other Ettes and had light spars, like *Ninette*. She was a fast boat and pointed better than other Ettes.

It was sad to see the final demise of the yachts, centreboard class and – ultimately – the Ettes. The yachts and the Ettes – good sea-boats that they were – looked a fine sight while sailing and were very enjoyable to sail.

facing page
Four Ette-class boats at the start of a race,
c. 1950.

Regattas

Regattas have always been popular along the south-west coast of Ireland. Held at the various coastal towns and villages, they provided great entertainment for all those interested in the sea and boating. Each town or village held its own regatta, and the one held in Castletownshend was regarded as one of the best. On the quay, music was played on a gramophone and relayed through loudspeakers at high volume. In some places, there were dancing competitions for the young and not-so-young, there was a greasy pole on which competitors tried to knock each other into the water with soggy pillows, and there was a sailing race for all boats that could sail, regardless of age or size. The start of this race was conducted from a committee-boat moored on the starting line, with race officials trying to get all the boats on the starting line at the same time, in line, and facing in the right direction. When this had been achieved, one of the officials, armed with a fully loaded 12-bore shotgun, fired the weapon without looking where it was pointing and many an unwary seagull or cormorant was shot down. The winner of the race was decided by a rough handicap. There was also a swimming race and a race in which a duck had to be caught.

The highlight of the day was the six-oared gig race, which was taken very seriously and was subject to much betting. The crews, which had been practicing hard all summer, were super fit. Naturally, most of them were fishermen, but sometimes a farmer pulled an oar if he was good enough. The race was a long one. In Castlehaven, the course was a line from Reen Pier to a buoy moored off Reen Point at the mouth of the harbour and back to the finishing line, which was roughly the same as the starting line. There was only one buoy for all competing boats to round, so it was important to reach the buoy first and round it before any other boat, otherwise there was a strong chance of a collision.

In bygone days, Castletownshend combined with Myross and raced against teams from Glandore, Schull, Sherkin Island and Baltimore. Interest in these regattas began to wane in the 1950s. However, they were

facing page
Castlehaven Rowing Club veteran men's crew, 1988.

revived in 1995 when the newly formed South West Cork Yawl Racing Association, under the auspices of the Irish Coastal Rowing Federation, started to hold regattas at the villages and towns where they were held before. These regattas now took a very different and more professional form. Gone were the swimming races, sailing races and all the other competitions. All racing was, and is to this day, between four-oared yawls with crews of all ages, ranging from the under-12s to the veteran men and women – that is, those over 45 years of age. Instead of there being only one buoy for all boats to round, there is now a buoy for each boat and these buoys are colour-coded.

In order to compete in these regattas, Castletownshend was given an old and heavy yawl which unfortunately never did well. So, in 1997, Castletownshend Rowing Club – which had been established in 1995 – decided to have a new yawl built. This was carried out by an excellent boat-builder in Kinsale. This new boat was named *The Hurricane*, and she took part in most of the races in all regattas that year, and exceeded all expectations by winning a number of trophies. Although she is immensely strong, she is light enough for four men to carry. Her ribs are oak and all her other timbers, including the thwarts, are mahogany. She is carvel-built and has no keel so she can turn fast at a buoy. The oar-gates are stainlesssteel and the oars are made of carbon-fibre.

Castletownshend, like most of the other coastal villages, has at least ten crews, so many families both in the village and outlying parish have at least one member as part of a crew. Training is hard; during the summer, almost every evening and in all weathers, the crews are out training. Besides yawls from Castletownshend, Schull, Union Hall (Myross) and Glandore, other places have formed rowing clubs and take part in regattas – places such as Rosscarbery, Galley Head, Bantry,

Kilmacsimon and Courtmacsherry. However, the championship regattas are held in Castletownshend, Baltimore, Schull, Glandore and Union Hall. There is a great team spirit in Castletownshend and especially within the rowing cub, with the result that *The Hurricane* is winning more races each year, and nearly every team has won at least one trophy in the county championships, county finals and the All-Ireland championships.

In 2001, the Irish Coastal Rowing Federation decided that all yawls were to be made of fibreglass, with a length of 24 feet instead of the present 21 feet. These new boats are heavier and their character and 'feel' not the same as the existing wooden boats. The reason for this decision was in order to make all boats equal.

In 2002, Margaret Warren very kindly gave her boat-house on the Western Quay to the rowing club on a ninety-nine-year lease. It was a magnificent gesture on the part of Margaret Warren, and is very much appreciated not only by the members of Castletownshend Rowing Club, but also by everyone in the village. The club will now have a very fine building to store its boats, train the crews throughout the year, hold meetings and display its many trophies.

In 1998, the All-Ireland Coastal Rowing Championships were held at Kinsale. The author was in the Castletownshend Rowing Club veteran men's team when it won a bronze medal for finishing third in its race. To qualify for this team, a man had to be over forty-five years old; the author was sixty-seven.

Visiting Yachts

Castlehaven has always been a favourite anchorage for visiting yachts as it is very sheltered and the bottom has good holding for anchoring. There is no harbour-master so there are no dues, and boats may anchor almost anywhere they like. Although there is no marina or fuel available, yachts can get water from the quay, and in the village there is a shop, post office and three pubs – in one, a good meal can be had. One of the earliest yachts to visit Castlehaven of which there is a record was a fine old schooner called *Shearwater*, which used to anchor there between the wars. She was English and probably built in the late 1800s. Another frequent visitor was *Shira*, which was sailed round from Parknasilla by a family that lived there. No yachts visited Castlehaven during the Second World War, and it was not until the 1970s that they began to visit in any number.

Nowadays, around 800 yachts visit Castlehaven each summer and, apart from Ireland, they come from France, England, the Isle of Man, Wales, Scotland, Belgium, Holland, Germany, the US and even Australia and New Zealand. (Some years ago, a lovely wooden yacht called in and anchored. She was crewed by a man and his wife; they had built her in New Zealand, sailed her to Rio de Janeiro, then across the Atlantic, and their first port of call was Castlehaven. She had no engine as the man's wife had insisted on putting a bathtub in the engine's space.) Most of the yachts calling today are modern and made of fibreglass, but some that visit are old and beautiful and made of timber. All these yachts, both ancient and modern, come in many different shapes and sizes; sloops, cutters, ketches, yawls and schooners. *Asgard II*, the Irish sail-training ship, is a regular visitor, with a crew of boys and girls under training. Of course, there are a number of motor-sailers and fast motor-boats, but the majority are yachts.

Another frequent visitor to Castlehaven is *Deerhound*, from Crosshaven. She is a lovely 51-foot ketch with tan sails, and has a number of single-handed transatlantic races under her keel. A few years ago, her owner, Colin Chapman – when returning single-handed

*Cruise-in-company
yachts in Castlehaven,
1997.*

from Marble Head – exhausted and battered, called in to Castlehaven, his first port of call; he stayed for a few days before continuing on to Crosshaven.

In 1977, the Irish Cruising Club, the Royal Cork Yacht Club, the Royal Cruising Club, the Clyde Cruising Club and the Cruising Club of America combined forces so that their members could take part in a 'cruise-in-company' along the south coast of Ireland, calling at various towns and villages. This cruise was such a success that it was decided to repeat the event every ten years. The harbour was always a fine sight whenever the event took place, as up to 100 yachts of various vintages and sizes took part, and they anchored either singly or several of them rafted up together and dressed overall. The number of yachts increased at every 'cruise-in-company', and it was decided to split the fleet, as some places, like Castlehaven, could not safely hold such large numbers. The next event will be held in 2007.

Every year over the Whit weekend, the Kinsale Yacht Club holds a race from Kinsale to Castlehaven which finishes across a line from the Rocket House flagstaff to a mark on the other side of the harbour. The yachts from this race only stay for an hour or two before heading back to Kinsale.

Our Boats

I must go down to the seas again, to the lonely sea and the sky, And all I ask is a tall ship and a star to steer her by

'Sea Fever' by John Masefield

We never got round to owning a tall ship but we did, at different times, own two small and beautiful yachts whose names were *Happy Days* and *Accolade*. *Happy Days* was made of timber and had been converted from a National 18 by a man in Cork. He did a fine job on her by putting on a deck, adding a small bowsprit and building a cabin that had a small galley and could sleep two people. Her cockpit was roomy and there was space for a couple of dogs under a thwart. Her draught was 2 feet, but when her centre-plate was fully lowered, another 2 feet were added. This was needed as she was somewhat over-canvassed. Although she was a sloop, she had two jibs: a light-weather one and a heavy-weather one, and both had roller reefing. She was a lovely boat and wonderful to sail.

Accolade was different. Unlike *Happy Days*, she was made of fibreglass and had bilge-keels. She also was a sloop but had more space below – she was able to sleep two people in comfort and four at a pinch. Her cockpit was smaller than that of *Happy Days*, but it was self-draining which made life easier. She sailed well except when going about, when the jib had to be backed to help her bow round (one of the disadvantages of bilge-keels).

We also owned two punts: the *Punt* and the *Barge*. The *Punt* was a lovely wooden, clinker-built boat of 15 feet. Built in Hegarty's Boatyard at Oldcourt, she was the predecessor of many similar punts in Castlehaven. Her bows had a nice flare which kept her dry except when under power in a choppy sea. The *Barge* came from Leap and was in a poor state of repair when we bought her. She was 12 feet long and had a clinker-built fibreglass hull and, like the *Punt*, was a delight to row.

Happy Days has since returned to Cork Harbour, from where she originated, and *Accolade* has a new owner in Baltimore. The *Barge* is still in Castlehaven with a new owner – Dick Kelly of Castletownshend. The *Punt* is also still to be found in Castlehaven.

Sadly, there are only a few pleasure boats left in Castlehaven whose owners live permanently in Castletownshend. Apart from punts and motor-boats, there are three sailing boats: *Gull*, a Wayfarer and *Ninette*.

At the
End of the Day

One of the best times in Castlehaven was at the end of a day when we had been for a good sail or had a picnic on some deserted strand. There is not even a smudge of cloud in the sky, and the wind, gradually dying, is from the south-west. The cacophony of din from outboards, jet-skis and motor-boats has died, and the only sounds are from gulls, a slight surge and draw of the sea on rocks and our boat pushing her way through the water. On our port quarter, the sun slowly sets, and to starboard, we pass Reen Point where the *Santa Anna Maria* was wrecked in that gale in 1628, and where so many Spanish sailors from the *Leon De Oro* lie buried. Then, the long stretch of strands and coves leading away to Reen Pier, with Raheen Castle in the background. To port, we pass Castlehaven Haul, Battery Point or Bullane, from where Spanish guns battered *Warspite*; Castlehaven Strand, where the early village was situated and where Admiral Zubiar's flagship was sunk by Admiral Leveson at the Battle of Castlehaven; Faill Dick, from where people got gravel for their drives; Poul Girm, which is good for bathing but always cold; Dutchman's Cove, where the Dutch ship, laden with timber, was wrecked; the Point Strand, then the Rocket House, built on the site of the old coastguard station, with its flagstaff. All these places have other stories to tell and have survived, over countless years, all that the elements could throw at them.

The light of the harbour changes and, as dusk approaches, we are reminded of that old Irish prayer:

The deep peace of the flowing air be always with you
The deep peace of the quiet earth be always with you
The deep peace of the running wave be always with you
The deep peace of the Son of Peace be always with you.

A sudden flurry of activity as we gybe, luff up into the wind and, hopefully, bring the boat to rest alongside her mooring buoy, which we pick up and secure, and put her to bed ready for another day.

facing page
Schooner anchored by the League (date unknown).

Glossary & Bibliography

Glossary

1 nautical mile 6080 feet.

1 land mile 5280 feet.

1 cable 200 yards.

1 fathom 6 feet.

Ballast Additional weight carried in a vessel to give her stability.

Barge A flat-bottomed coastal-trading vessel.

Bermuda Rig A sail plan in which the main and mizzen are triangular in shape.

Bottle-screw A rigging screw used to adjust any rigging equipment for tension.

Bowsprit A spar projecting over the bow of a vessel to which the forestay is attached.

Broach The tendency of a sailing vessel to fly up into the wind when sailing off the wind.

Capstan A cylindrical barrel, fitted to the foredeck, used for lifting heavy objects.

Chinese Gybe A type of wild and premeditated gybe when the boom lifts over the lee side of a vessel while the gaff does not follow.

Clew The name given to the lower aftermost corner of a fore-and-aft sail.

Cutter A dinker-built ship's boat of 32 feet with a single mast and twelve oars *or* a sailing boat with two head sails.

Dipping Lug A rig in which the forward end of the yard carrying the sail projects forward of the mast entailing lowering the sail about 3 feet and dipping the yard round the mast whenever the boat goes about.

Fore-and-aft Rig The arrangement of sails in a vessel so that the luffs of the sails abut the mast or are attached to stays.

Gudgeon The metal plate carrying the eye bolted onto the sternpost or transom of a boat.

Gunter of Standing Rig A sail which is cut with a short luff and a long leech. The head of the sail is attached to a yard which, when hoisted, is an extension to the mast.

Halyard Rope or wire used to hoist sails.

Kicking Strap A rope or strap that runs from a point on a dinghy's boom to the foot of the mast. It helps to prevent the boom from rising when off the wind.

Leech The after edge of a fore-and-aft sail.

Lighter A boat without her own means of propulsion used for conveyance of cargo from ship to shore or vice versa.

Loose-footed Sail A sail that is attached to a boom only by its tack and clew.

Pintle A vertical metal pin attached to the leading edge of a rudder.

Ribs Another name for the frames or timbers of a wooden vessel.

Sheet A single line used for trimming a sail.

Tack The name given to the forward and lowest corner of a fore-and-aft sail *or* the operation of bringing a sailing vessel head to wind and across it so as to bring the wind on the opposite side.

Thole Pin A wooden pin fixed to the gunwhale of a boat to which an oar is attached.

Thwart A transverse seat in a boat on which an oarsman sits.

Transom The athwart ship timbers that are bolted to the sternpost of a vessel to give her a flat stern.

Yawl In a yawl, the mizzen mast is stepped abaft the rudder head. In a ketch, it is forward of the rudder head. Yawl is also a name given to a boat that has four oars.

Bibliography

Admiralty Chart 5011, dated 1846

A Seaman's Pocket Book

Ordnance Survey Office, Dublin

The Oxford Companion to Ships and the Sea

Irish Sword, 1965

Globe, 7 November 1805